The Education of the Child

Ellen Key

1st WORLD
LIBRARY
Literary Society

The Education of the Child

Ellen Key

© 1st World Library – Literary Society, 2004
PO Box 2211
Fairfield, IA 52556
www.1stworldlibrary.org
First Edition

LCCN: 2004091182

Softcover ISBN: 1-59540-628-X
eBook ISBN: 1-59540-728-6

Purchase *"The Education of the Child"*
as a traditional bound book at:
www.1stWorldLibrary.org/purchase.asp?ISBN=1-59540-628-X

1st World Library Literary Society is a nonprofit
organization dedicated to promoting literacy by:

- Creating a free internet library accessible from any computer worldwide.
- Hosting writing competitions and offering book publishing scholarships.

Readers interested in supporting literacy
through sponsorship, donations or
membership please contact:
literacy@1stworldlibrary.org
Check us out at: www.1stworldlibrary.org

The Education of the Child
contributed by the Mahaney Family
in support of
1st World Library Literary Society

INTRODUCTORY NOTE

Edward Bok, Editor of the "Ladies' Home Journal," writes:

"Nothing finer on the wise education of the child has ever been brought into print. To me this chapter is a perfect classic; it points the way straight for every parent and it should find a place in every home in America where there is a child."

The Education of the Child

Goethe showed long ago in his Werther a clear understanding of the significance of individualistic and psychological training, an appreciation which will mark the century of the child. In this work he shows how the future power of will lies hidden in the characteristics of the child, and how along with every fault of the child an uncorrupted germ capable of producing good is enclosed. "Always," he says, "I repeat the golden words of the teacher of mankind, 'if ye do not become as one of these,' and now, good friend, those who are our equals, whom we should look upon as our models, we treat as subjects; they should have no will of their own; do we have none? Where is our prerogative? Does it consist in the fact that we are older and more experienced? Good God of Heaven! Thou seest old and young children, nothing else. And in whom Thou hast more joy, Thy Son announced ages ago. But people believe in Him and do not hear Him - that, too, is an old trouble, and they model their children after themselves." The same criticism might be applied to our present educators, who constantly have on their tongues such words as evolution, individuality, and natural tendencies, but do not heed the new commandments in which they say they believe. They continue to educate as if they believed still in the natural depravity of man, in original sin, which may be bridled, tamed, suppressed, but not changed. The new belief is really equivalent to Goethe's thoughts given above, i.e., that almost every fault is but a hard shell enclosing the germ of virtue. Even men of modern times still follow in education the old rule of medicine, that evil must be driven out by evil, instead of the new method, the system of allowing nature quietly and slowly to help itself, taking care only that the surrounding conditions help the work of nature. This is education.

Neither harsh nor tender parents suspect the truth expressed by Carlyle when he said that the marks of a noble and original temperament are wild, strong emotions, that must be controlled by a discipline as hard as steel. People either strive to root out passions altogether, or they abstain from teaching the child to get them under control.

To suppress the real personality of the child, and to supplant it with another personality continues to be a pedagogical crime common to those who announce loudly that education should only develop the real individual nature of the child.

They are still not convinced that egoism on the part of the child is justified. Just as little are they convinced of the possibility that evil can be changed into good.

Education must be based on the certainty that faults cannot be atoned for, or blotted out, but must always have their consequences. At the same time, there is the other certainty that through progressive evolution, by slow adaptation to the conditions of environment they may be transformed. Only when this stage is reached will education begin to be a science and art. We will then give up all belief in the miraculous effects of

Ellen Key

sudden interference; we shall act in the psychological sphere in accordance with the principle of the indestructibility of matter. We shall never believe that a characteristic of the soul can be destroyed. There are but two possibilities. Either it can be brought into subjection or it can be raised up to a higher plane.

Madame de Stael's words show much insight when she says that only the people who can play with children are able to educate them. For success in training children the first condition is to become as a child oneself, but this means no assumed childishness, no condescending baby-talk that the child immediately sees through and deeply abhors. What it does mean is to be as entirely and simply taken up with the child as the child himself is absorbed by his life. It means to treat the child as really one's equal, that is, to show him the same consideration, the same kind confidence one shows to an adult. It means not to influence the child to be what we ourselves desire him to become but to be influenced by the impression of what the child himself is; not to treat the child with deception, or by the exercise of force, but with the seriousness and sincerity proper to his own character. Somewhere Rousseau says that all education has failed in that nature does not fashion parents as educators nor children for the sake of education. What would happen if we finally succeeded in following the directions of nature, and recognised that the great secret of education lies hidden in the maxim, "do not educate"?

Not leaving the child in peace is the greatest evil of present-day methods of training children. Education is determined to create a beautiful world externally and internally in which the child can grow. To let him move about freely in this world until he comes into contact with the permanent boundaries of another's right will be the end of the education of the future. Only then will adults really obtain a deep insight into the souls of children, now an almost inaccessible kingdom. For it is a natural instinct of self-preservation which causes the child to bar the educator from his innermost nature. There is the person who asks rude questions; for example, what is the child thinking about? a question which almost invariably is answered with a black or a white lie. The child must protect himself from an educator who would master his thoughts and inclinations, or rudely handle them, who without consideration betrays or makes ridiculous his most sacred feelings, who exposes faults or praises characteristics before strangers, or even uses an open-hearted, confidential confession as an occasion for reproof at another time.

The statement that no human being learns to understand another, or at least to be patient with another, is true above all of the intimate relation of child and parent in which, understanding, the deepest characteristic of love, is almost always absent.

Parents do not see that during the whole life the need of peace is never greater than in the years of childhood, an inner peace under all external unrest. The child has to enter into relations with his own infinite world, to conquer it, to make it the object of his dreams. But what does he experience? Obstacles, interference, corrections, the whole livelong day. The child is always required to leave something alone, or to do something different, to find something different, or want something different from what he does, or finds, or wants. He is always shunted off in another direction from that towards which his own character is leading

Ellen Key

him. All of this is caused by our tenderness, vigilance, and zeal, in directing, advising, and helping the small specimen of humanity to become a complete example in a model series.

I have heard a three-year-old child characterised as "trying" because he wanted to go into the woods, whereas the nursemaid wished to drag him into the city. Another child of six years was disciplined because she had been naughty to a playmate and had called her a little pig, - a natural appellation for one who was always dirty. These are typical examples of how the sound instincts of the child are dulled. It was a spontaneous utterance: of the childish heart when a small boy, after an account of the heaven of good children, asked his mother whether she did not believe that, after he had been good a whole week in heaven, he might be allowed to go to hell on Saturday evening to play with the bad little boys there.

The child felt in its innermost consciousness that he had a right to be naughty, a fundamental right which is accorded to adults; and not only to be naughty, but to be naughty in peace, to be left to the dangers and joys of naughtiness.

To call forth from this "unvirtue" the complimentary virtue is to overcome evil with good. Otherwise we overcome natural strength by weak means and obtain artificial virtues which will not stand the tests which life imposes.

It seems simple enough when we say that we must overcome evil with good, but practically no process is more involved, or more tedious, than to find actual means to accomplish this end. It is much easier to say what one shall not do than what one must do to change self-will into strength of character, slyness into prudence, the desire to please into amiability, restlessness into personal initiative. It can only be brought about by recognising that evil, in so far as it is not atavistic or perverse, is as natural and indispensable as the good, and that it becomes a permanent evil only through its one-sided supremacy.

The educator wants the child to be finished at once, and perfect. He forces upon the child an unnatural degree of self-mastery, a devotion to duty, a sense of honour, habits that adults get out of with astonishing rapidity. Where the faults of children are concerned, at home and in school, we strain at gnats, while children daily are obliged to swallow the camels of grown people.

The art of natural education consists in ignoring the faults of children nine times out of ten, in avoiding immediate interference, which is usually a mistake, and devoting one's whole vigilance to the control of the environment in which the child is growing up, to watching the education which is allowed to go on by itself. But educators who, day in and day out, are consciously transforming the environment and themselves are still a rare product. Most people live on the capital and interest of an education, which perhaps once made them model children, but has deprived them of the desire for educating themselves. Only by keeping oneself in constant process of growth, under the constant influence of the best things in one's own age, does one become a companion half-way good enough for one's children.

To bring up a child means carrying one's soul in one's

hand, setting one's feet on a narrow path, it means never placing ourselves in danger of meeting the cold look on the part of the child that tells us without words that he finds us insufficient and unreliable. It means the humble realisation of the truth that the ways of injuring the child are infinite, while the ways of being useful to him are few. How seldom does the educator remember that the child, even at four or five years of age, is making experiments with adults, seeing through them, with marvellous shrewdness making his own valuations and reacting sensitively to each impression. The slightest mistrust, the smallest unkindness, the least act of injustice or contemptuous ridicule, leave wounds that last for life in the finely strung soul of the child. While on the other side unexpected friendliness, kind advances, just indignation, make quite as deep an impression on those senses which people term as soft as wax but treat as if they were made of cowhide.

Relatively most excellent was the old education which consisted solely in keeping oneself whole, pure, and honourable. For it did not at least depreciate personality, although it did not form it. It would be well if but a hundredth part of the pains now taken by parents were given to interference with the life of the child and the rest of the ninety and nine employed in leading, without interference, in acting as an unforeseen, an invisible providence through which the child obtains experience, from which he may draw his own conclusions. The present practice is to impress one's own discoveries, opinions, and principles on the child by constantly directing his actions. The last thing to be realised by the educator is that he really has before him an entirely new soul, a real self whose first and chief right is to think over the things with which he comes in contact. By a new soul he understands only a new generation of an old humanity to be treated with a fresh dose of the old remedy. We teach the new souls not to steal, not to lie, to save their clothes, to learn their lessons, to economise their money, to obey commands, not to contradict older people, say their prayers, to fight occasionally in order to be strong. But who teaches the new souls to choose for themselves the path they must tread? Who thinks that the desire for this path of their own can be so profound that a hard or even mild pressure towards uniformity can make the whole of childhood a torment.

The child comes into life with the inheritance of the preceding members of the race; and this inheritance is modified by adaptation to the environment. But the child shows also individual variations from the type of the species, and if his own character is not to disappear during the process of adaptation, all self-determined development of energy must be aided in every way and only indirectly influenced by the teacher, who should understand how to combine and emphasise the results of this development.

Interference on the part of the educator, whether by force or persuasion, weakens this development if it does not destroy it altogether.

The habits of the household, and the child's habits in it must be absolutely fixed if they are to be of any value. Amiel truly says that habits are principles which have become instincts, and have passed over into flesh and blood. To change habits, he continues, means to attack life in its very essence, for life is only a web of habits.

Why does everything remain essentially the same from generation to generation? Why do highly civilised

Christian people continue to plunder one another and call it exchange, to murder one another en masse, and call it nationalism, to oppress one another and call it statesmanship?

Because in every new generation the impulses supposed to have been rooted out by discipline in the child, break forth again, when the struggle for existence - of the individual in society, of the society in the life of the state - begins. These passions are not transformed by the prevalent education of the day, but only repressed. Practically this is the reason why not a single savage passion has been overcome in humanity. Perhaps man-eating may be mentioned as an exception. But what is told of European ship companies or Siberian prisoners shows that even this impulse, under conditions favourable to it, may be revived, although in the majority of people a deep physical antipathy to man-eating is innate. Conscious incest, despite similar deviations, must also be physically contrary to the majority, and in a number of women, modesty - the unity between body and soul in relation to love - is an incontestable provision of nature. So too a minority would find it physically impossible to murder or steal. With this list I have exhausted everything which mankind, since its conscious history began, has really so intimately acquired that the achievement is passed on in its flesh and blood. Only this kind of conquest can really stand up against temptation in every form.

A deep physiological truth is hidden in the use of language when one speaks of unchained passions; the passions, under the prevailing system of education, are really only beasts of prey imprisoned in cages.

While fine words are spoken about individual development, children are treated as if their personality had no purpose of its own, as if they were made only for the pleasure, pride, and comfort of their parents; and as these aims are best advanced when children become like every one else, people usually begin by attempting to make them respectable and useful members of society.

But the only correct starting point, so far as a child's education in becoming a social human being is concerned, is to treat him as such, while strengthening his natural disposition to become an individual human being.

The new educator will, by regularly ordered experience, teach the child by degrees his place in the great orderly system of existence; teach him his responsibility towards his environment. But in other respects, none of the individual characteristics of the child expressive of his life will be suppressed, so long as they do not injure the child himself, or others. The right balance must be kept between Spencer's definition of life as an adaptation to surrounding conditions, and Nietzsche's definition of it as the will to secure power.

In adaptation, imitation certainly plays a great role, but individual exercise of power is just as important. Through adaptation life attains a fixed form; through exercise of power, new factors.

Thoughtful people, as I have already stated, talk a good deal about personality. But they are, nevertheless, filled with doubts when their children are not just like all other children; when they cannot show in their offspring all the ready-made virtues required by society. And so they drill their children, repressing in childhood the natural instincts which will have freedom when they are grown. People still hardly realise how new human beings are formed; therefore the old types constantly repeat themselves in the same circle, - the fine young men, the sweet girls, the respectable officials, and so on. And new types with higher ideals, - travellers on unknown paths, thinkers of yet unthought thoughts, people capable of the crime of inaugurating new ways, - such types rarely come into existence among those who are well brought up.

Nature herself, it is true, repeats the main types constantly. But she also constantly makes small deviations. In this way different species, even of the human race, have come into existence. But man himself does not yet see the significance of this natural law in his own higher development. He wants the feelings, thoughts, and judgments already stamped with approval to be reproduced by each new generation. So we get no new individuals, but only more or less prudent, stupid, amiable, or bad-tempered examples of the genus man. The still living instincts of the ape, double, in the case of man, the effect of heredity. Conservatism is for the present stronger in mankind than the effort to produce new types. But this last characteristic is the most valuable. The educator should do anything but advise the child to do what everybody does. He should rather rejoice when he sees in the child tendencies to deviation. Using other people's opinion as a standard results in subordinating one's self to their will. So we become a part of the great mass, led by the Superman through the strength of his will, a will which could not have mastered strong personalities. It has been justly remarked that individual peoples, like the English, have attained the greatest political and social freedom, because the personal feeling of independence is far in excess of freedom in a legal form. Accordingly legal freedom has been constantly growing.

For the progress of the whole of the species, as well as of society, it is essential that education shall awake the feeling of independence; it should invigorate and favour the disposition to deviate from the type in those cases where the rights of others are not affected, or where deviation is not simply the result of the desire to draw attention to oneself. The child should be given the chance to declare conscientiously his independence of a customary usage, of an ordinary feeling, for this is the foundation of the education of an individual, as well as the basis of a collective conscience, which is the only kind of conscience men now have. What does having an individual conscience mean? It means submitting voluntarily to an external law, attested and found good by my own conscience. It means unconditionally heeding the unwritten law, which I lay upon myself, and following this inner law even when I must stand alone against the whole world.

It is a frequent phenomenon, we can almost call it a regular one, that it is original natures, particularly talented beings, who are badly treated at home and in school. No one considers the sources of conduct in a child who shows fear or makes a noise, or who is absorbed in himself, or who has an impetuous nature. Mothers and teachers show in this their pitiable incapacity for the most elementary part in the art of education, that is, to be able to see with their own eyes, not with pedagogical doctrines in their head.

I naturally expect in the supporters of society, with their conventional morality, no appreciation of the significance of the child's putting into exercise his own powers. Just as little is this to be expected of those Christian believers who think that human nature must be brought to repentance and humility, and that the sinful body, the unclean beast, must be tamed with the rod, - a theory which the Bible is brought to support.

I am only addressing people who can think new thoughts and consequently should cease using old methods of education. This class may reply that the new ideas in education cannot be carried out. But the obstacle is simply that their new thoughts have not made them into new men; the old man in them has neither repose, nor time, nor patience, to form his own soul, and that of the child, according to the new thoughts.

Those who have "tried Spencer and failed," because Spencer's method demands intelligence and patience, contend that the child must be taught to obey, that truth lies in the old rule, "As the twig is bent the tree is inclined."

BENT is the appropriate word, bent according to the old ideal which extinguishes personality, teaches humility and obedience. But the new ideal is that man, to stand straight and upright, must not be bent at all only supported, and so prevented from being deformed by weakness.

One often finds, in the modern system of training, the crude desire for mastery still alive and breaking out when the child is obstinate. "You won't!" say father and mother; "I will teach you whether you have a will.

I will soon drive self-will out of you." But nothing can be driven out of the child; on the other hand, much can be scourged into it which should be kept far away.

Only during the first few years of life is a kind of drill necessary, as a pre-condition to a higher training. The child is then in such a high degree controlled by sensation, that a slight physical pain or pleasure is often the only language he fully understands. Consequently for some children discipline is an indispensable means of enforcing the practice of certain habits. For other children, the stricter methods are entirely unnecessary even at this early age, and as soon as the child can remember a blow, he is too old to receive one.

The child must certainly learn obedience, and, besides, this obedience must be absolute. If such obedience has become habitual from the tenderest age, a look, a word, an intonation is enough to keep the child straight. The dissatisfaction of those who are bringing him up can only be made effective when it falls as a shadow in the usual sunny atmosphere of home. And if people refrain from laying the foundations of obedience while the child is small, and his naughtiness is entertaining, Spencer's method undoubtedly will be found unsuitable after the child is older and his caprice disagreeable.

With a very small child, one should not argue, but act consistently and immediately. The effort of training should be directed at an early period to arrange the experiences in a consistent whole of impressions according to Rousseau and Spencer's recommendation. So certain habits will become impressed in the flesh and blood of the child.

Constant crying on the part of small children must be corrected when it has become clear that the crying is not caused by illness or some other discomfort, - discomforts against which crying is the child's only weapon. Crying is now ordinarily corrected by blows. But this does not master the will of the child, and only produces in his soul the idea that older people strike small children, when small children cry. This is not an ethical idea. But when the crying child is immediately isolated, and it is explained to him at the same time that whoever annoys others must not be with them; if this isolation is the absolute result, and cannot be avoided, in the child's mind a basis is laid for the experience that one must be alone when one makes oneself unpleasant or disagreeable. In both cases the child is silenced by interfering with his comfort; but one type of discomfort is the exercise of force on his will; the other produces slowly the self-mastery of the will, and accomplishes this by a good motive. One method encourages a base emotion, fear. The other corrects the will in a way that combines it with one of the most important experiences of life. The one punishment keeps the child on the level of the animal. The other impresses upon him the great principle of human social life, that when our pleasure causes displeasure to others, other people hinder us from following our pleasures; or withdraw themselves from the exercise of our self-will. It is necessary that small children should accustom themselves to good behaviour at table, etc. If every time an act of naughtiness is repeated, the child is immediately taken away, he will soon learn that whoever is disagreeable to others must remain alone. Thus a right application is made of a right principle. Small children, too, must learn not to touch what belongs to other people. If every time anything is touched without permission, children lose their freedom of action one way or another, they soon learn that a condition of their free action is not to injure others.

It is quite true, as a young mother remarked, that empty Japanese rooms are ideal places in which to bring up children. Our modern crowded rooms are, so far as children are concerned, to be condemned. During the year in which the real education of the child is proceeding by touching, tasting, biting, feeling, and so on, every moment he is hearing the cry, "Let it alone." For the temperament of the child as well as for the development of his powers, the best thing is a large, light nursery, adorned with handsome lithographs, wood-cuts, and so on, provided with some simple furniture, where he may enjoy the fullest freedom of movement. But if the child is there with his parents and is disobedient, a momentary reprimand is the best means to teach him to reverence the greater world in which the will of others prevails, the world in which the child certainly can make a place for himself but must also learn that every place occupied by him has its limits.

If it is a case of a danger, which it is desirable that the child should really dread, we must allow the thing itself to have an alarming influence. When a mother strikes a child because he touches the light, the result is that he does this again when the mother is away. But let him burn himself with the light, then he is certain to leave it alone. In riper years when a boy misuses a knife, a toy, or something similar, the loss of the object for the time being must be the punishment. Most boys would prefer corporal punishment to the loss of their favourite possession. But only the loss of it will be a real education through experience of one of the inevitable rules of life, an experience which cannot be too strongly impressed.

We hear parents who have begun with Spencer and then have taken to corporal punishment declare that when children are too small to repair the clothing which they have torn there must be some other kind of punishment. But at that age they should not be punished at all for such things. They should have such simple and strong clothes that they can play freely in them. Later on, when they can be really careful, the natural punishment would be to have the child remain at home if he is careless, has spotted his clothes, or torn them. He must be shown that he must help to put his clothes in good condition again, or that he will be compelled to buy what he has destroyed carelessly with money earned by himself. If the child is not careful, he must stay at home, when ordinarily allowed to go out, or eat alone if he is too late for meals. It may be said that there are simple means by which all the important habits of social life may become a second nature. But it is not possible in all cases to apply Spencer's method. The natural consequences occasionally endanger the health of the child, or sometimes are too slow in their action. If it seems necessary to interfere directly, such action must be consistent, quick, and immutable. How is it that the child learns very soon that fire burns? Because fire does so always. But the mother who at one time strikes, at another threatens, at another bribes the child, first forbids and then immediately after permits some action; who does not carry out her threat, does not compel obedience, but constantly gabbles and scolds; who sometimes acts in one way and just as often in another, has not learned the effective educational methods of the fire.

The old-fashioned strict training that in its crude way gave to the character a fixed type rested on its consistent qualities. It was consistently strict, not as at present a lax hesitation between all kinds of pedagogical methods and psychological opinions, in which the child is thrown about here and there like a ball, in the hands of grown people; at one time pushed forward, then laughed at, then pushed aside, only to be brought back again, kissed till it, is disgusted, first ordered about, and then coaxed. A grown man would become insane if joking Titans treated him for a single day as a child is treated for a year. A child should not be ordered about, but should be just as courteously addressed as a grown person in order that he may learn courtesy. A child should never be pushed into notice, never compelled to endure caresses, never over-whelmed with kisses, which ordinarily torment him and are often the cause of sexual hyperaesthesia. The child's demonstrations of affection should be reciprocated when they are sincere, but one's own demonstrations should be reserved for special occasions. This is one of the many excellent maxims of training that are disregarded. Nor should the child be forced to express regret in begging pardon and the like. This is excellent training for hypocrisy. A small child once had been rude to his elder brother and was placed upon a chair to repent his fault. When the mother after a time asked if he was sorry, he answered, "Yes," with emphasis, but as the mother saw a mutinous sparkle in his eyes she felt impelled to ask, "Sorry for what?" and the youngster broke out, "Sorry that I did not call him a liar besides." The mother was wise enough on this occasion, and ever after, to give up insisting on repentance.

Spontaneous penitence is full of significance, it is a

deeply felt desire for pardon. But an artificial emotion is always and everywhere worthless. Are you not sorry? Does it make no difference to you that your mother is ill, your brother dead, your father away from home? Such expressions are often used as an appeal to the emotions of children. But children have a right to have feelings, or not have them, and to have them as undisturbed as grown people. The same holds good of their sympathies and antipathies. The sensitive feelings of children are constantly injured by lack of consideration on the part of grown people, their easily stimulated aversions are constantly being brought out. But the sufferings of children through the crudeness of their elders belong to an unwritten chapter of child psychology. Just as there are few better methods of training than to ask children, when they have behaved unjustly to others, to consider whether it would be pleasant for them to be treated in that way, so there is no better corrective for the trainer of children than the habit of asking oneself, in question small and great, - Would I consent to be treated as I have just treated my child? If it were only remembered that the child generally suffers double as much as the adult, parents would perhaps learn physical and psychical tenderness without which a child's life is a constant torment.

As to presents, the same principle holds good as with emotions and marks of tenderness. Only by example can generous instincts be provoked. Above all the child should not be allowed to have things which he immediately gives away. Gifts to a child should always imply a personal requital for work or sacrifice. In order to secure for children the pleasure of giving and the opportunity of obtaining small pleasures and enjoyments, as well as of replacing property of their own or of others which they may have destroyed, they should at an early age be accustomed to perform seriously certain household duties for which they receive some small remuneration. But small occasional services, whether volunteered or asked for by others, should never be rewarded. Only readiness to serve, without payment, develops the joy of generosity. When the child wants to give away something, people should not make a presence of receiving it. This produces the false conception in his mind that the pleasure of being generous can be had for nothing. At every step the child should be allowed to meet the real experiences of life; the thorns should never be plucked from his roses. This is what is least understood in present-day training. Thus we see reasonable methods constantly failing. People find themselves forced to "afflictive" methods which stand in no relation with the realities of life. I mean, above all, what are still called means of education, instead of means of torture, - blows.

Many people of to-day defend blows, maintaining that they are milder means of punishment than the natural consequences of an act; that blows have the strongest effect on the memory, which effect becomes permanent through association of ideas.

But what kinds of association? Is it not with physical pain and shame? Gradually, step by step, this method of training and discipline has been superseded in all its forms. The movement to abolish torture, imprisonment, and corporal punishment failed for a long time owing to the conviction that they were indispensable as methods of discipline. But the child, people answer, is still an animal, he must be brought up as an animal. Those who talk in this way know nothing of children nor of animals. Even animals can be trained without striking them, but they can only be trained by men who have become men themselves.

Others come forward with the doctrine that terror and pain have been the best means of educating mankind, so the child must pursue the same road as humanity. This is an utter absurdity. We should also, on this theory, teach our children, as a natural introduction to religion, to practice fetish worship. If the child is to reproduce all the lower development stages of the race, he would be practically depressed beneath the level which he has reached physiologically and psychologically through the common inheritance of the race. If we have abandoned torture and painful punishments for adults, while they are retained for children, it is because we have not yet seen that their soul life so far as a greater and more subtle capacity for suffering is concerned has made the same progress as that of adult mankind. The numerous cases of child suicide in the last decade were often the result of fear of corporal punishment; or have taken place after its administration. Both soul and body are equally affected by this practice. Where this is not the result, blows have even more dangerous consequences. They tend to dull still further the feeling of shame, to increase the brutality or cowardice of the person punished. I once heard a child pointed out in a school as being so unruly that it was generally agreed he would be benefited by a flogging. Then it was discovered that his father's flogging at home had made him what he was. If statistics were prepared of ruined sons, those who had been flogged would certainly be more numerous than those who had been pampered.

Society has gradually given up employing retributive punishments because people have seen that they neither awaken the feeling of guilt, nor act as a deterrent, but on the contrary retribution applied by equal to equal brutalises the ideas of right, hardens the temper, and stimulates the victim to exercise the same violence towards others that has been endured by himself. But other rules are applied to the psychological processes of the child. When a child strikes his small sister the mother strikes him and believes that he will see and understand the difference between the blows he gets and those he gives, that he will see that the one is a just punishment and the other vicious conduct. But the child is a sharp logician and feels that the action is just the same, although the mother gives it a different name.

Corporal punishment was long ago admirably described by Comenius, who compared an educator using this method with a musician striking a badly tuned instrument with his fist, instead of using his ears and his hands to put it into tune.

These brutal attacks work on the active sensitive feelings, lacerating and confusing them. They have no educative power on all the innumerable fine processes in the life of the child's soul, on their obscurely related combinations.

In order to give real training, the first thing after the second or third year is to abandon the very thought of a blow among the possibilities of education. It is best if parents, as soon as the child is born, agree never to strike him, for if they once begin with this convenient and easy method, they continue to use corporal discipline even contrary to their first intention, because they have failed while using such punishment to develop the child's intelligence.

If people do not see this it is no more use to speak to them of education than it would be to talk to a cannibal about the world's peace.

But as these savages in educational matters are often civilised human beings in other respects, I should like to request them to think over the development of marriage from the time when man wooed with a club and when woman was regarded as the soulless property of man, only to be kept in order by blows, a view which continued to be held until modern times. Through a thousand daily secret influences, our feelings and ideas have been so transformed that these crude conceptions have disappeared, to the great advantage of society and the individual. But it may be hard to awaken a pedagogical savage to the conviction that, in quite the same way, a thousand new secret and mighty influences will change our crude methods of education, when parents once come to see that parenthood must go through the same transformation as marriage, before it attains to a noble and complete development.

Only when men realise that whipping a child belongs to the same low stage of civilisation as beating a woman, or a servant, or as the corporal punishment of soldiers and criminals, will the first real preparation begin of the material from which perhaps later an educator may be formed.

Corporal punishment was natural in rough times. The body is tangible; what affects it has an immediate and perceptible result. The heat of passion is cooled by the blows it administers; in a certain stage of development blows are the natural expression of moral indignation, the direct method by which the moral will impresses itself on beings of lower capacities. But it has since been discovered that the soul may be impressed by spiritual means, and that blows are just as demoralising for the one who gives them as for the one who receives them.

The educator, too, is apt to forget that the child in many cases has as few moral conceptions as the animal or the savage. To punish for this - is only a cruelty, and to punish by brutal methods is a piece of stupidity. It works against the possibility of elevating the child beyond the level of the beast or the savage. The educator to whose mind flogging never presents itself, even as an occasional resource, will naturally direct his whole thought to finding psychological methods of education. Administering corporal punishment demoralises and stupefies the educator, for it increases his thoughtlessness, not his patience, his brutality, not his intelligence.

A small boy friend of mine when four years old received his first punishment of this kind; happily it was his only one. As his nurse reminded him in the evening to say his prayers he broke out, "Yes, to-night I really have something to tell God," and prayed with deep earnestness, "Dear God, tear mamma's arms out so that she cannot beat me any more."

Nothing would more effectively further the development of education than for all flogging pedagogues to meet this fate. They would then learn to educate with the head instead of with the hand. And as to public educators, the teachers, their position could be no better raised than by legally forbidding a blow to be administered in any school under penalty of final loss of position.

That people who are in other respects intelligent and sensitive continue to defend flogging, is due to the fact that most educators have only a very elementary conception of their work. They should constantly keep before them the feelings and impressions of their own childhood in dealing with children. The most frequent as well as the most dangerous of the numerous mistakes made in handling children is that people do not remember how they felt themselves at a similar age, that they do not regard and comprehend the feelings of the child from their own past point of view. The adult laughs or smiles in remembering the punishments and other things which caused him in his childhood anxious days or nights, which produced the silent torture of the child's heart, infinite despondency, burning indignation, lonely fears, outraged sense of justice, the terrible creations of his imagination, his absurd shame, his unsatisfied thirst for joy, freedom, and tenderness. Lacking these beneficent memories, adults constantly repeat the crime of destroying the childhood of the new generation, - the only time in life in which the guardian of education can really be a kindly providence. So strongly do I feel that the unnecessary sufferings of children are unnatural as well as ignoble that I experience physical disgust in touching the hand of a human being that I know has struck a child; and I cannot close my eyes after I have heard a child in the street threatened with corporal punishment.

Blows call forth the virtues of slaves, not those of freemen. As early as Walther von der Vogelweide, it was known that the honourable man respects a word more than a blow. The exercise of physical force delivers the weak and unprotected into the hands of the strong. A child never believes in his heart, though he may be brought to acknowledge verbally, that the blows were due to love, that they were administered because they were necessary. The child is too keen not to know that such a "must" does not exist, and that love can express itself in a better way.

Lack of self-discipline, of intelligence, of patience, of personal effort - these are the corner-stones on which corporal punishment rests. I do not now refer to the system of flogging employed by miserable people year in and year out at home, or, particularly in schools, that of beating children outrageously, or to the limits of brutality. I do not mean even the less brutal blows administered by undisciplined teachers and parents, who avenge themselves in excesses of passion or fatigue or disgust, - blows which are simply the active expression of a tension of nerves, a detestable evidence of the want of self-discipline and selfculture. Still less do I refer to the cruelties committed by monsters, sexual perverts, whose brutal tendencies are stimulated by their disciplinary power and who use it to force their victims to silence, as certain criminal trials have shown.

I am only speaking of conscientious, amiable parents and teachers who, with pain to themselves, fulfil what they regard as their duty to the child. These are accustomed to adduce the good effects of corporal discipline as a proof that it cannot be dispensed with. The child by being whipped is, they say, not only made good but freed from his evil character, and shows by his whole being that this quick and summary method of punishment has done more than talks, and patience, and the slowly working penalties of experience. Examples are adduced to prove that only this kind of punishment breaks down obstinacy, cures the habit of lying and the like. Those who adopt this system do not perceive that they have only succeeded, through this momentarily effective means, in repressing the external expression of an evil will. They have not succeeded in transforming the will itself. It requires constant vigilance, daily self-discipline, to create an ever higher capacity for the discovery of intelligent methods. The fault that is repressed is certain to appear on every occasion when the child dares to show it. The educator who finds in corporal punishment a short way to get rid of trouble, leads the child a long way round, if we have the only real development in view, namely that which gradually strengthens the child's capacity for self-control.

I have never heard a child over three years old threatened with corporal punishment without noticing that this wonderfully moral method had an equally bad influence on parents and children. The same can be said of milder kinds of folly, coaxing children by external rewards. I have seen some children coaxed to take baths and others compelled by threats. But in neither case was their courage, or self-control, or strength of will increased. Only when one is able to make the bath itself attractive is that energy of will developed that gains a victory over the feeling of fear or discomfort and produces a real ethical impression, viz., that virtue is its own reward. Wherever a child is deterred from a bad habit or fault by corporal punishment, a real ethical result is not reached. The child has only learnt to fear an unpleasant conse-quence, which lacks real connection with the thing itself, a consequence it well knows could have been absent. Such fear is as far removed as heaven from the conviction that the good is better than the bad. The child soon becomes convinced that the disagreeable accompaniment is no necessary result of the action, that by greater cleverness the punishment might have been avoided. Thus the physical punishment increases deception not morality. In the history of humanity the effect of the teaching about hell and fear of hell illustrates the sort of morality produced in children's souls by corporal punishment, that inferno of child-hood. Only with the greatest trouble, slowly and unconsciously, is the conviction of the superiority of the good established. The good comes to be seen as more productive of happiness to the individual himself and his environment. So the child learns to love the good. By teaching the child that punishment is a consequence drawn upon oneself he learns to avoid the cause of punishment.

Despite all the new talk of individuality the greatest mistake in training children is still that of treating the "child" as an abstract conception, as an inorganic or personal material to be formed and transformed by the hands of those who are educating him. He is beaten, and it is thought that the whole effect of the blow stops at the moment when the child is prevented from being bad. He has, it is thought, a powerful reminder against future bad behaviour. People no not suspect that this violent interference in the physical and psychical life of the child may have lifelong effects. As far back as forty years ago, a writer showed that corporal punishment had the most powerful somatic stimulative effects. The flagellation of the Middle Ages is known to have had such results; and if I could publish what I have heard from adults as to the effect of corporal punishment on them, or what I have observed in children, this alone would be decisive in doing away with such punishment in its crudest form. It very deeply influences the personal modesty of the child.

This should be preserved above everything as the main factor in the development of the feeling of purity. The father who punishes his daughter in this way deserves to see her some day a "fallen woman." He injures her instinctive feeling of the sanctity of her body, an instinct which even in the case of a small child can be passionately profound. Only when every infringement of sanctity (forcible caressing is as bad as a blow) evokes an energetic, instinctive repulsion, is the nature of the child proud and pure. Children who strike back when they are punished have the most promising characters of all.

Numerous are the cases in which bodily punishment can occasion irremediable damage, not suspected by the person who administers it, though he may triumphantly declare how the punishment in the specific case has helped. Most adults feel free to tell how a whipping has injured them in one way or another, but when they take up the training of their own children they depend on the effect of such chastisement.

What burning bitterness and desire for vengeance, what canine fawning flattery, does not corporal punishment call forth. It makes the lazy lazier, the obstinate more obstinate, the hard, harder. It strengthens those two emotions, the root of almost all evil in the world, hatred and fear. And as long as blows are made synonymous with education, both of these emotions will keep their mastery over men.

One of the most frequent occasions for recourse to this punishment is obstinacy, but what is called obstinacy is only fear or incapacity. The child repeats a false answer, is threatened with blows, and again repeats it just because he is afraid not to say the right thing. He is struck and then answers rightly. This is a triumph of education; refractoriness is overcome. But what has happened? Increased fear has led to a strong effort of thought, to a momentary increase of self-control. The next day the child will very likely repeat the fault. Where there is real obstinacy on the part of children, I know of cases when corporal punishment has filled them with the lust to kill, either themselves or the person who strikes them. On the other hand I know of others, where a mother has brought an obstinate child to repentance and self-mastery by holding him quietly and calmly on her knees.

How many untrue confessions have been forced by fear of blows; how much daring passion for action, spirit of adventure, play of fancy, and stimulus to discovery has been repressed by this same fear. Even where blows do not cause lying, they always hinder absolute straightforwardness and the down-right personal courage to show oneself as one is. As long as the word "blow" is used at all in a home, no perfect honour will be found in children. So long as the home and the school use this method of education, brutality will be developed in the child himself at the cost of humanity. The child uses on animals, on his young brothers and sisters, on his comrades, the methods applied to himself. He puts in practice the same argument, that "badness" must be cured with blows. Only children accustomed to be treated mildly, learn to see that influence can be gained without using force. To see this is one of man's privileges, sacrificed by man through descending to the methods of the brute. Only by the child seeing his teacher always and everywhere abstaining from the use of actual force, will he come himself to despise force on all those occasions which do not involve the defence of a weaker person against physical superiority. The foundation of the desire for war is to be sought for less in the war games than in the teachers' rod.

To defend corporal discipline, children's own statements are brought in evidence, they are reported as saying they knew they deserved such discipline in order to be made good. There is no lower example of hypocrisy in human nature than this. It is true the child may be sincere in other cases in saying that he feels that through punishment he has atoned for a fault which was weighing upon his conscience. But this is really the foundation of a false system of ethics, the kind which still continues to be preached as Christian, namely; that a fault may be atoned for by sufferings which are not directly connected with the fault. The basis of the new morality is just the opposite as I have already shown. It teaches that no fault can be atoned for, that no one can escape the results of his actions in any way.

Untruthfulness belongs to the faults which the teacher thinks he must most frequently punish with blows. But there is no case in which this method is more dangerous.

When the much-needed guide-book for parents is published, the well-known story of George Washington and the hatchet must appear in it, accompanied by the remark which a clever ten-year-old child added to the anecdote: "It is no trouble telling the truth when one has such a kind father."

I formerly divided untruthfulness into unwilling, shameless, and imaginative lies. A short time ago I ran across a much better division of lying; first "cold" lies, that is, fully conscious untruthfulness which must be punished, and "hot" lies; the expression of an excited temperament or of a vigorous fancy. I agree with the author of this distinction that the last should not be punished but corrected, though not with a pedantic rule of thumb measure, based on how much it exceeds or falls short of truth. It is to be cured by ridicule, a dangerous method of education in general, but useful when one observes that this type of untruthfulness threatens to develop into real untrustworthiness. In dealing with these faults we are very strict towards children, so strict that no lawyer, no politician, no journalist, no poet, could exercise his profession if the same standard were applied to them as to children.

The white lie is, as a French scientist has shown, partly caused by pure morbidness, partly through some defect in the conception. It is due to an empty space, a dead point in memory, or in consciousness, that produces a defective idea or gives one no idea at all of what has happened. In the affairs of everyday life the adults are often mistaken as to their intentions or acts. They may have forgotten about their actions, and it requires a strong effort of memory to call them back into their minds; or they suggest to themselves that they have done, or not done, something. In all of these cases, if they were forced to give a distinct answer, they would lie. In every case of this kind, where a child is concerned, the lie is assumed to be a conscious one, and when on being submitted to a strict cross-examination, he hesitates, becomes confused, and blushes, it is looked upon as a proof that he knows he has been telling an untruth, although as a rule there has been no instance of untruthfulness, except the finally extorted confession from the child that he has lied. Yet in all these complicated psychological problems, corporal punishment is treated as a solution.

The child who never hears lying at home, who does not see exaggerated weight placed on small, merely external things, who is not made cowardly by fear, who hears conscious lies always spoken of with contempt, will get out of the habit of untruthfulness simply by psychological means. First he will find that untruthfulness causes astonishment, and a repetition of it, scorn and lack of confidence. But these methods should not be applied to untruthfulness caused by distress or by richness of imagination; or to such cases as originate from the obscure mental ideas noted above, ideas whose connection with one another the child cannot make clear to himself. The cold untruth on the other hand, must be punished; first by going over it with the child, then letting him experience its effect in lack of confidence, which will only be restored when the child shows decided improvement in this regard. It is of the greatest importance to show children full and unlimited confidence, even though one quietly maintains an attitude of alert watchfulness; for continuous and undeserved mistrust is just as demoralising as blind and easy confidence.

No one who has been beaten for lying learns by it to love truth. The accuracy of this principle is illustrated by adults who despise corporal punishment in their childhood yet continue to tell untruths by word and deed. Fear may keep the child from technical untruth, but fear also produces untrustworthiness. Those who have been beaten in childhood for lying have often suffered a serious injury immeasurably greater than the direct lie. The truest men I ever knew lie voluntarily and involuntarily; while others who might never be caught in a lie are thoroughly false.

This corruption of personality begins frequently at the tenderest age under the influence of early training. Children are given untrue motives, half-true information; are threatened, admonished. The child's will, thought, and feeling are oppressed; against this treatment dishonesty is the readiest method of defence. In this way educators who make truth their highest aim, make children untruthful. I watched a child who was severely punished for denying something he had unconsciously done, and noted how under the influence of this senseless punishment he developed extreme dissimulation.

Truthfulness requires above everything unbroken determination; and many nervous little liars need nourishing food and life in the open air, not blows. A great artist, one of the few who live wholly according to the modern principles of life, said to me on one occasion: "My son does not know what a lie is, nor what a blow is. His step-brother, on the other hand, lied when he came into our house; but lying did not work in the atmosphere of calm and freedom. After a year the habit disappeared by itself, only because it always met with deep astonishment."

This makes me, in passing, note one of the other many mistakes of education, viz., the infinite trouble taken in trying to do away with a fault which disappears by itself. People take infinite pains to teach small children to speak distinctly who, if left to themselves, would learn it by themselves, provided they were always spoken to distinctly. This same principle holds good of numerous other things, in children's attitude and behaviour, that can be left simply to a good example and to time. One's influence should be used in impressing upon the child habits for which a foundation must be laid at the very beginning of his life.

There is another still more unfortunate mistake, the mistake of correcting and judging by an external effect produced by the act, by the scandal it occasions in the environment. Children are struck for using oaths and improper words the meaning of which they do not understand; or if they do understand, the result of strictness is only that they go on keeping silence in matters in which sincerity towards those who are bringing them up is of the highest importance. The very thing the child is allowed to do uncorrected at home, is not seldom corrected if it happens away from home. So the child gets a false idea that it is not the thing that deserves punishment, but its publicity. When a mother is ashamed of the bad behaviour of her son she is apt to strike him - instead of striking her own breast! When an adventurous feat fails he is beaten, but he is praised when successful. These practices produce demoralisation. Once in a wood I saw two parents laughing while the ice held on which their son was sliding; when it broke suddenly they threatened to whip him. It required strong self-control in order not to say to this pair that it was not the son who deserved punishment but themselves.

On occasions like these, parents avenge their own fright on their children. I saw a child become a coward because an anxious mother struck him every time he fell down, while the natural result inflicted on the child would have been more than sufficient to increase his carefulness. When misfortune is caused by disobedience, natural alarm is, as a rule, enough to prevent a repetition of it. If it is not sufficient blows have no restraining effect; they only embitter. The boy finds that adults have forgotten their own period of childhood; he withdraws himself secretly from this abuse of power, provided strict treatment does not succeed in totally depressing the level of the child's will and obstructing his energies.

This is certainly a danger, but the most serious effect of corporal punishment is that it has established an unethical morality as its result. Until the human being has learnt to see that effort, striving, development of power, are their own reward, life remains an unbeautiful affair. The debasing effects of vanity and ambition, the small and great cruelties produced by injustice, are all due to the idea that failure or success sets the value to deeds and actions.

A complete revolution in this crude theory of value must come about before the earth can become the scene of a happy but considerate development of power on the part of free and fine human beings. Every contest decided by examinations and prizes is ultimately an immoral method of training. It awakens only evil passions, envy and the impression of injustice on the one side, arrogance on the other. After I had during the course of twenty years fought these school examinations, I read with thorough agreement a short time ago, Ruskin's views on the subject. He believed that all competition was a false basis of stimulus, and every distribution of prizes a false means. He thought that the real sign of talent in a boy, auspicious for his future career, was his desire to work for work's sake. He declared that the real aim of instruction should be to show him his own proper and special gifts, to strengthen them in him, not to spur him on to an empty competition with those who were plainly his superiors in capacity.

Moreover it ought not to be forgotten that success and failure involve of themselves their own punishment and their own reward, the one bitter, the other sweet enough to secure in a natural way increased strength, care, prudence, and endurance. It is completely unnecessary for the educator to use, besides these, some special punishments or special rewards, and so pervert the conceptions of the child that failure seems to him to be a wrong, success on the other hand as the right.

No matter where one turns one's gaze, it is notorious that the externally encouraging or awe-inspiring means of education, are an obstacle to what are the chief human characteristics, courage in oneself and goodness to others.

A people whose education is carried on by gentle means only (I mean the people of Japan), have shown that manliness is not in danger where children are not hardened by corporal punishment. These gentle means are just as effective in calling forth selfmastery and consideration. These virtues are so imprinted on children, at the tenderest age, that one learns first in Japan what attraction considerate kindliness bestows upon life. In a country where blows are never seen, the first rule of social intercourse is not to cause discomfort to others. It is told that when a foreigner in Japan took up a stone to throw it at a dog, the dog did not run. No one had ever thrown a stone at him. Tenderness towards animals is the complement in that country of tenderness in human relationship, a tenderness whose result is observed, among other effects, in a relatively small number of crimes against life and security.

War, hunting for pleasure, corporal discipline, are nothing more than different expressions of the tiger nature still alive in man. When the rod is thrown away, and when, as some one has said, children are no longer boxed on their ears but are given magnifying glasses and photographic cameras to increase their capacity for life and for loving it, instead of learning to destroy it, real education in humanity will begin.

For the benefit of those who are not convinced that corporal punishment can be dispensed with in a manly education, by so remote and so distant an example as Japan, I should like to mention a fact closer to us. Our Germanic forefathers did not have this method of education. It was introduced with Christianity. Corporal discipline was turned into a religious duty, and as late as the seventeenth century there were intelligent men who flogged their children once a week as a part of spiritual guardianship. I once asked our great poet, Victor Rydberg, and he said that he had found no proof that corporal punishment was usual among the Germans in heathen times. I asked him whether he did not believe that the fact of its absence had encouraged the energetic individualism and manliness in the Northern peoples. He thought so, and agreed with me. Finally, I might note from our own time, that there are many families and schools, our girls' schools for example, and also boys' schools in some countries, where corporal punishment is never used. I know a family with twelve children whose activity and capacity are not damaged by bringing them under the rule of duty alone. Corporal punishment is never used in this home; a determined but mild mother has taught the children to obey voluntarily, and has known how to train their wills to self-control.

By "voluntary obedience," I do not mean that the child is bound to ask endless questions for reasons, and to dispute them before he obeys. A good teacher never gives a command without there being some good reason, but whether the child is convinced or not, he must always obey, and if he asks "why" the answer is very simple; every one, adults as well as children, must obey the right and must submit to what cannot be avoided. The great necessity in life must be imprinted in childhood. This can be done without harsh means by training the child, even previous to his birth, by cultivating one's self-control, and after his birth by never giving in to a child's caprices. The rule is, in a few cases, to work in opposition to the action of the child, but in other cases work constructively; I mean provide the child with material to construct his own personality and then let him do this work of construction. This is, in brief, the art of education. The worst of all educational methods are threats. The only effective admonitions are short and infrequent ones. The greatest skill in the educator is to be silent for the moment and then so reprove the fault, indirectly, that the child is brought to correct himself or make himself the object of blame. This can be done by the instructor telling something that causes the child to compare his own conduct with the hateful or admirable types of behaviour about which he hears information. Or the educator may give an opinion which the child must take to himself although it is not applied directly to him.

On many occasions a forceful display of indignation on the part of the elder person is an excellent punishment, if the indignation is reserved for the right moment. I know children to whom nothing was more frightful than their father's scorn; this was dreaded.

Children who are deluged with directions and religious devotions, who receive an ounce of morality in every cup of joy, are most certain to be those who will revolt against all this. Nearly every thinking person feels that the deepest educational influences in his life have been indirect; some good advice not given to him directly; a noble deed told without any direct reference. But when people come themselves to train others they forget all their own personal experience.

The strongest constructive factor in the education of a human being is the settled, quiet order of home, its peace, and its duty. Open-heartedness, industry, straightforwardness at home develop goodness, desire to work, and simplicity in the child. Examples of artistic work and books in the home, its customary life on ordinary days and holidays, its occupations and its pleasures, should give to the emotions and imagination of the child, periods of movement and repose, a sure contour and a rich colour. The pure, warm, clear atmosphere in which father, mother, and children live together in freedom and confidence; where none are kept isolated from the interests of the others; but each possesses full freedom for his own personal interest; where none trenches on the rights of others; where all are willing to help one another when necessary, - in this atmosphere egoism, as well as altruism, can attain their richest development, and individuality find its just freedom. As the evolution of man's soul advances to undreamed-of possibilities of refinement, of capacity, of profundity; as the spiritual life of the generation becomes more manifold in its combinations and in its distinctions; the more time one has for observing the wonderful and deep secrets of existence, behind the visible, tangible, world of sense, the more will each new generation of children show a more refined and a more consistent mental life. It is impossible to attain this result under the torture of the crude methods in our present home and school training. We need new homes, new schools, new marriages, new social relations, for those new souls who are to feel, love, and suffer, in ways infinitely numerous that we now can not even name. Thus they will come to understand life; they will have aspirations and hopes; they will believe; they will pray. The conceptions of religion, love, and art, all these must be revolutionised so radically, that one now can only surmise what new forms will be created in future generations. This transformation can be helped by the training of the present, by casting aside the withered foliage which now covers the budding possibilities of life.

The house must once more become a home for the souls of children, not for their bodies alone. For such homes to be formed, that in their turn will mould children, the children must be given back to the home. Instead of the study preparation at home for the school taking up, as it now does, the best part of a child's life, the school must get the smaller part, the home the larger part. The home will have the responsibility of so using the free time as well on ordinary days as on holidays, that the children will really become a part of the home both in their work and in their pleasures. The children will be taken from the school, the street, the factory, and restored to the home. The mother will be given back from work outside, or from social life to the children. Thus natural training in the spirit of Rousseau and Spencer will be realised; a training for life, by life at home.

Such was the training of Old Scandanavia; the direct

share of the child in the work of the adult, in real labours and dangers, gave to the life of our Scandanavian forefathers (with whom the boy began to be a man at twelve years of age), unity, character, and strength. Things specially made for children, the anxious watching over all their undertakings, support given to all their steps, courses of work and pleasure specially prepared for children, - these are the fundamental defects of our present day education. An eighteen-yearold girl said to me a short time ago, that she and other girls of the same age were so tired of the system of vigilance, protection, amusement, and pampering at school and at home, that they were determined to bring up their own children in hunger, corporal discipline, and drudgery.

One can understand this unfortunate reaction against an artificial environment, the environment in which children and young people of the present grow up; an existence that evokes a passionate desire for the realities of life, for individual action at one's own risk and responsibility, instead of being, as is now the case, at home and in the school, the object of another's care.

What is required, above all, for the children of the present day, is to be assigned again real home occupations, tasks they must do conscientiously, habits of work arranged for week days and holidays without oversight, in every case where the child can help himself. Instead of the modern school child having a mother and servants about him to get him ready for school and to help him to remember things, he should have time every day before school to arrange his room and brush his clothes, and there should be no effort to make him remember what is connected with the school. The home and the school should combine together systematically to let the child suffer for the results of his own negligence.

Just the reverse of this system rules to-day. Mothers learn their children's lessons, invent plays for them, read their story books to them, arrange their rooms after them, pick up what they have let fall, put in order the things they have left in confusion, and in this and in other ways, by protective pampering and attention, their desire for work, their endurance, the gifts of invention and imagination, qualities proper to the child, become weak and passive. The home now is only a preparation for school. In it, young people growing up, are accustomed to receive services, without performing any on their part. They are trained to be always receptive instead of giving something in return. Then people are surprised at a youthful generation, selfish and unrestrained, pressing forward shamelessly on all occasions before their elders, crudely unresponsive in respect of those attentions, which in earlier generations were a beautiful custom among the young.

To restore this custom, all the means usually adopted now to protect the child from physical and psychical dangers and inconveniences, will have to be removed. Throw the thermometer out of the window and begin with a sensible course of toughening; teach the child to know and to bear natural pain. Corporal punishment must be done away with not because it is painful but because it is profoundly immoral and hopelessly unsuitable. Repress the egoistic demands of the child when he interferes with the work or rest of others; never let him either by caresses or by nagging usurp the rights of grown people; take care that the servants do not work against what the parents are trying to insist on in this and in other matters.

We must begin in doing for the child in certain ways a thousand times more and in others a hundred thousand times less. A beginning must be made in the tenderest age to establish the child's feeling for nature. Let him live year in and year out in the same country home; this is one of the most significant and profound factors in training. It can be held to even where it is now neglected. The same thing holds good of making a choice library, commencing with the first years of life; so that the child will have, at different periods of his life, suitable books for each age; not as is now often the case, get quite spoilt by the constant change of summer excursions, by worthless children's books, and costly toys. They should never have any but the simplest books; the so-called classical ones. They should be amply provided with means of preparing their own playthings. The worst feature of our system are the playthings which imitate the luxury of grown people. By such objects the covetous impulse of the child for acquisition is increased, his own capacity for discovery and imagination limited, or rather, it would be limited if children with the sound instinct of preservation, did not happily smash the perfect playthings, which give them no creative opportunity, and themselves make new playthings from fir cones, acorns, thorns, and fragments of pottery, and all other sorts of rubbish which can be transformed into objects of great price by the power of the imagination.

To play with children in the right way is also a great art. It should never be done if children do not themselves know what they are going to do; it should always be a special treat for them as well as their elders. But the adults must always on such occasions, leave behind every kind of educational idea and go completely into the child's world of thought and imagination. No attempt should be made to teach them at these times anything else but the old satisfactory games. The experiences derived from these games about the nature of the children, who are stimulated in one direction or another by the game, must be kept for later use.

Games in this way increase confidence between children and adults. They learn to know their elders better. But to allow children to turn all the rooms into places to play in, and to demand constantly that their elders shall interest themselves in them, is one of the most dangerous species of pampering common to the present day. The children become accustomed to selfishness and mental dependence. Besides this constant educational effort brings with it the dulling of the child's personality. If children were free in their own world, the nursery, but out of it had to submit to the strict limits imposed by the habits, wills, work, and repose of parents, their requirements and their wishes, they would develop into a stronger and more considerate race than the youth of the present day. It is not so much talking about being considerate, but the necessity of considering others, of really helping oneself and others, that has an educational value. In earlier days, children were quiet as mice in the presence of elder persons. Instead of, as they do now, breaking into a guest's conversation, they learned to listen. If the conversation of adults is varied, this can be called one of the best educational methods for children. The ordinary life of children, under the old system, was lived in the nursery where they received their most important training from an old faithful servant and from one another. From their parents they received corporal punishment, sometimes a caress. In comparison with this system, the present way of parents and children living together would be absolute progress, if parents could but abstain from explaining, advising, improving, influencing every thought and every expression. But all spiritual, mental, and bodily protective rules make the child now indirectly selfish, because everything centres about him and therefore he is kept in a constant state of irritation. The six-yearold can disturb the conversation of the adult, but the twelve-year-old is sent to bed about eight o'clock, even when he, with wide open eyes, longs for a conversation that might be to him an inspiring stimulus for life.

Certainly some simple habits so far as conduct and order, nourishment and sleep, air and water, clothing and bodily movement, are concerned, can be made the foundations for the child's conceptions of morality. He cannot be made to learn soon enough that bodily health and beauty must be regarded as high ethical characteristics, and that what is injurious to health and beauty must be regarded as a hateful act. In this sphere, children must be kept entirely independent of custom by allowing the exception to every rule to have its valid place. The present anxious solicitude that children should eat when the clock strikes, that they get certain food at fixed meals, that they be clothed according to the degree of temperature, that they go to bed when the clock strikes, that they be protected from every drop of unboiled water and every extra piece of candy, this makes them nervous, irritable slaves of habit. A reasonable toughening process against the inequalities, discomforts, and chances of life, constitutes one of the most important bases of joy of living and of strength of temper. In this case too, the behaviour of the person who gives the training, is the best means of teaching children to smile at small contretemps, things which would throw a cloud over the sun, if one got into the habit of treating them as if they were of great importance. If the child sees the parent doing readily an unpleasant duty, which he honestly recognises as unpleasant; if he sees a parent endure trouble or an unexpected difficulty easily, he will be in honour bound to do the like. Just as children without many words learn to practice good deeds when they see good deeds practiced about them; learn to enjoy the beauty of nature and art when they see that adults enjoy them, so by living more beautifully, more nobly, more moderately, we speak best to children. They are just as receptive to impressions of this kind as they are careless of those made by force.

Since this is my alpha and omega in the art of education, I repeat now what I said at the beginning of this book and half way through it. Try to leave the child in peace; interfere directly as seldom as possible; keep away all crude and impure impressions; but give all your care and energy to see that personality, life itself, reality in its simplicity and in its nakedness, shall all be means of training the child.

Make demands on the powers of children and on their capacity for self-control, proportionate to the special stage of their development, neither greater nor lesser demands than on adults. But respect the joys of the child, his tastes, work, and time, just as you would those of an adult. Education will thus become an infinitely simple and infinitely harder art, than the education of the present day, with its artificialised existence, its double entry morality, one morality for the child, and one for the adult, often strict for the child and lax for the adult and vice versa. By treating the child every moment as one does an adult human being we free education from that brutal arbitrariness, from those over-indulgent protective rules, which have transformed him. Whether parents act as if children existed for their benefit alone, or whether the parents give up their whole lives to their children, the result is alike deplorable. As a rule both classes know equally little of the feelings and needs of their children. The one class are happy when the children are like themselves, and their highest ambition is to produce in their children a successful copy of their own thoughts, opinions, and ideals. Really it ought to pain them very much to see themselves so exactly copied. What life expected from them and required from them was just the opposite - a richer combination, a better creation, a new type, not a reproduction of that which is already exhausted. The other class strive to model their chilrden not according to themselves but according to their ideal of goodness. They show their love by their willingness to extinguish their own personalities for their children's sake. This they do by letting the children feel that everything which concerns them stands in the foreground. This should be so, but only indirectly.

The concerns of the whole scheme of life, the ordering of the home, its habits, intercourse, purposes, care for the needs of children, and their sound development, must stand in the foreground. But at present, in most cases, children of tender years, as well as those who are older, are sacrificed to the chaotic condition of the home. They learn self-will without possessing real freedom, they live under a discipline which is spasmodic in its application.

When one daughter after another leaves home in order

to make herself independent they are often driven to do it by want of freedom, or by the lack of character in family life. In both directions the girl sees herself forced to become something different, to hold different opinions, to think different thoughts, to act contrary to the dictates of her own being. A mother happy in the friendship of her own daughter, said not long ago that she desired to erect an asylum for tormented daughters. Such an asylum would be as necessary as a protection against pampering parents as against those who are overbearing. Both alike, torture their children though in different ways, by not understanding the child's right to have his own point of view, his own ideal of happiness, his own proper tastes and occupation. They do not see that children exist as little for their parent's sake as parents do for their children's sake. Family life would have an intelligent character if each one lived fully and entirely his own life and allowed the others to do the same. None should tyrannise over, nor should suffer tyranny from, the other. Parents who give their home this character can justly demand that children shall accommodate themselves to the habits of the household as long as they live in it. Children on their part can ask that their own life of thought and feeling shall be left in peace at home, or that they be treated with the same consideration that would be given to a stranger. When the parents do not meet these conditions they themselves are the greater sufferers. It is very easy to keep one's son from expressing his raw views, very easy to tear a daughter away from her book and to bring her to a tea-party by giving her unnecessary occupations; very easy by a scornful word to repress some powerful emotion. A thousand similar things occur every day in good families through the whole world. But whenever we hear of young people speaking of their intellectual homelessness and sadness, we begin to understand why father and mother remain behind in homes from which the daughters have hastened to depart; why children take their cares, joys, and thoughts to strangers; why, in a word, the old and the young generation are as mutually dependent as the roots and flowers of plants, so often separate with mutual repulsion.

This is as true of highly cultivated fathers and mothers as of simple bourgeois or peasant parents. Perhaps, indeed, it may be truer of the first class, the latter torment their children in a naive way, while the former are infinitely wise and methodical in their stupidity. Rarely is a mother of the upper class one of those artists of home life who through the blitheness, the goodness, and joyousness of her character, makes the rhythm of everyday life a dance, and holidays into festivals. Such artists are often simple women who have passed no examinations, founded no clubs, and written no books. The highly cultivated mothers and the socially useful mothers on the other hand are not seldom those who call forth criticism from their sons. It seems almost an invariable rule that mothers should make mistakes when they wish to act for the welfare of their sons. "How infinitely valuable," say their children, "would I have found a mother who could have kept quiet, who would have been patient with me, who would have given me rest, keeping the outer world at a distance from me, with kindly soothing hands. Oh, would that I had had a mother on whose breast I could have laid my head, to be quiet and dream."

A distinguished woman writer is surprised that all of her well-thought-out plans for her children fail - those children in whom she saw the material for her passion

Ellen Key

for governing, the clay that she desired to mould.

The writer just cited says very justly that maternal unselfishness alone can perform the task of protecting a young being with wisdom and kindliness, by allowing him to grow according to his own laws. The unselfish mother, she says, will joyfully give the best of her life energy, powers of soul and spirit to a growing being and then open all doors to him, leaving him in the broad world to follow his own paths, and ask for nothing, neither thanks, nor praise, nor remembrance. But to most mothers may be applied the bitter exclamation of a son in the book just mentioned, "even a mother must know how she tortures another; if she has not this capacity by nature, why in the world should I recognise her as my mother at all."

Certain mothers spend the whole day in keeping their children's nervous system in a state of irritation. They make work hard and play joyless, whenever they take a part in it. At the present time, too, the school gets control of the child, the home loses all the means by which formerly it moulded the child's soul life and ennobled family life. The school, not father and mother, teaches children to play, the school gives them manual training, the school teaches them to sing, to look at pictures, to read aloud, to wander about out of doors; schools, clubs, sport and other pleasures accustom youth in the cities more and more to outside life, and a daily recreation that kills the true feeling for holiday. Young people, often, have no other impression of home than that it is a place where they meet society which bores them.

Parents surrender their children to schools in those years in which they should influence their minds.

When the school gives them back they do not know how to make a fresh start with the children, for they themselves have ceased to be young.

But getting old is no necessity; it is only a bad habit. It is very interesting to observe a face that is getting old. What time makes out of a face shows better than anything else what the man has made out of time. Most men in the early period of middle age are neither intellectually fat nor lean, they are hardened or dried up. Naturally young people look upon them with unsympathetic eyes, for they feel that there is such a thing as eternal youth, which a soul can win as a prize for its whole work of inner development. But they look in vain for this second eternal youth in their elders, filled with worldly nothingnesses and things of temporary importance.

With a sigh they exclude the "old people" from their future plans and they go out in the world in order to choose their spiritual parents.

This is tragic but just, for if there is a field on which man must sow a hundred-fold in order to harvest tenfold it is the souls of children.

When I began at five years of age to make a rag doll, that by its weight and size really gave the illusion of reality and bestowed much joy on its young mother, I began to think about the education of my future children. Then as now my educational ideal was that the children should be happy, that they should not fear. Fear is the misfortune of childhood, and the sufferings of the child come from the half-realised opposition between his unlimited possibilities of happiness and the way in which these possibilities are actually handled. It may be said that life, at every stage, is cruel in its treatment of our possibilities of happiness. But the difference between the sufferings of the adult from existence, and the sufferings of the child caused by adults, is tremendous. The child is unwilling to resign himself to the sufferings imposed upon him by adults and the more impatient the child is against unnecessary suffering, the better; for so much the more certainly will he some day be driven to find means to transform for himself and for others the hard necessities of life.

A poet, Rydberg, in our country who had the deepest intuition into child's nature, and therefore had the deepest reverence for it, wrote as follows: "Where we behold children we suspect there are princes, but as to the kings, where are they?" Not only life's tragic elements diminish and dam up its vital energies. Equally destructive is a parent's want of reverence for the sources of life which meet them in a new being. Fathers and mothers must bow their heads in the dust before the exalted nature of the child. Until they see that the word "child" is only another expression for the conception of majesty; until they feel that it is the future which in the form of a child sleeps in their arms, and history which plays at their feet, they will not understand that they have as little power or right to prescribe laws for this new being as they possess the power or might to lay down paths for the stars.

The mother should feel the same reverence for the unknown worlds in the wide-open eyes of her child, that she has for the worlds which like white blossoms are sprinkled over the blue orb of heaven; the father should see in his child the king's son whom he must serve humbly with his own best powers, and then the child will come to his own; not to the right of asking others to become the plaything of his caprices but to the right of living his full strong personal child's life along with a father and a mother who themselves live a personal life, a life from whose sources and powers the child can take the elements he needs for his own individual growth. Parents should never expect their own highest ideals to become the ideals of their child. The free-thinking sons of pious parents and the Christian children of freethinkers have become almost proverbial.

But parents can live nobly and in entire accordance to their own ideals which is the same thing as making children idealists. This can often lead to a quite different system of thought from that pursued by the parent.

As to ideals, the elders should here as elsewhere, offer with timidity their advice and their experience. Yes they should try to let the young people search for it as if they were seeking fruit hidden under the shadow of leaves. If their counsel is rejected, they must show neither surprise nor lack of self-control.

The query of a humourist, why he should do anything for posterity since posterity had done nothing for him, set me to thinking in my early youth in the most serious way. I felt that posterity had done much for its forefathers. It had given them an infinite horizon for the future beyond the bounds of their daily effort. We must in the child see the new fate of the human race; we must carefully treat the fine threads in the child's soul because these are the threads that one day will form the woof of world events. We must realise that every pebble by which one breaks into the glassy depths of the child's soul will extend its influence through centuries and centuries in ever widening circles. Through our fathers, without our will and without choice, we are given a destiny which controls the deepest foundation of our own being. Through our posterity, which we ourselves create, we can in a certain measure, as free beings, determine the future destiny of the human race.

By a realisation of all this in an entirely new way, by seeing the whole process in the light of the religion of development, the twentieth century will be the century of the child. This will come about in two ways. Adults will first come to an understanding of the child's character and then the simplicity of the child's character will be kept by adults. So the old social order will be able to renew itself.

Psychological pedagogy has an exalted ancestry. I will not go back to those artists in education called Socrates and Jesus, but I commence with the modern world. In the hours of its sunrise, in which we, who look back, think we see a futile Renaissance, then as now the spring flowers came up amid the decaying foliage. At this period there came a demand for the remodelling of education through the great figure of modern times, Montaigne, that skeptic who had so deep a reverence for realities. In his Essays, in his Letters to the Countess of Gurson, are found all of the elements for the education of the future. About the great German and Swiss specialists in pedagogy and psychology, Comenius, Basedow, Pestalozzi, Salzmann, Froebel, Herbart, I do not need to speak. I will only mention that the greatest men of Germany, Lessing, Herder, Goethe, Kant and others, took the side of natural training. In regard to England it is well known that John Locke in his Thoughts on Education, was a worthy predecessor of Herbert Spencer, whose book on education in its intellectual, moral, and physical relations, was the most noteworthy book on education in the last century.

It has been noted that Spencer in educational theory is indebted to Rousseau; and that in many cases, he has only said what the great German authorities, whom he certainly did not know, said before him. But this does not diminish Spencer's merit in the least. Absolutely new thoughts are very rare. Truths which were once new must be constantly renewed by being pronounced again from the depth of the ardent personal conviction of a new human being.

That rational thoughts on the subject of pedagogy as on other subjects, are constantly expressed and re-expressed, shows among other things that reasonable, or practically untried education has certain principles which are as axiomatic as those of mathematics. Every reasonable thinking man must as certainly discover anew these pedagogical principles, as he must discover anew the relation between the angles of a triangle. Spencer's book it is true has not laid again the foundation of education. It can rather be called the crown of the edifice founded by Montaigne, Locke, Rousseau, and the great German specialists in pedagogy. What is an absolutely novel factor in our times is the study of the psychology of the child, and the system of education that has developed from it.

In England, through the scientist Darwin, this new study of the psychology of the child was inaugurated. In Germany, Preyer contributed to its extension. He has done so partly by a comprehensive study of children's language, partly by collecting recollections of childhood on the part of the adult. Finally he experimented directly on the child, investigating his physical and psychical fatigue and endurance, acuteness of sensation, power, speed, and exactness in carrying out physical and mental tasks. He has studied his capacity of attention in emotions and in ideas at different periods of life. He has studied the speech of children, association of ideas in children, etc. During the study of the psychology of the child, scholars began to substitute for this term the expression "genetic psychology." For it was found that the big-genetic principle was valid for the development both of the psychic and the physical life. This principle means that the history of the species is repeated in the history of the individual; a truth substantiated in other spheres; in philology for example. The psychology of the child is of the same significance for general psychology as embryology is for anatomy. On the other hand, the description of savage peoples, of peoples in a natural condition, such as we find in Spencer's Descriptive Sociology or Weitz's Anthropology is extremely instructive for a right conception of the psychology of the child.

It is in this kind of psychological investigation that the greatest progress has been made in this century. In the great publication, Zeitschrift fur psychologie, etc., there began in 1894 a special department for the psychology of children and the psychology of education. In 1898, there were as many as one hundred and six essays devoted to this subject, and they are constantly increasing.

In the chief civilised countries this investigation has many distinguished pioneers, such as Prof. Wundt, Prof. T. H. Ribot, and others. In Germany this subject has its most important organ in the journal mentioned above. It numbers among its collaborators some of the most distinguished German physiologists and psychologists. As related to the same subject must be mentioned Wundt's Philosophischen Studien, and partly the Vierteljahrschrift fur Wissenschaftlichie Philosophie. In France, there was founded in 1894, the Annee Psychologique, edited by Binet and Beaunis, and also the Bibliotheque de Pedagogie et de Psychologie, edited by Binet. In England there are the journals, Mind and Brain.

Special laboratories for experimental psychology with psychological apparatus and methods of research are found in many places. In Germany the first to be founded was that of Wundt in the year 1878 at Leipzig. France has a laboratory for experimental psychology at Paris, in the Sorbonne, whose director is Binet; Italy, one in Rome. In America experimental psychology is zealously pursued. As early as 1894, there were in that country twenty-seven laboratories for experimental psychology and four journals. There should also be mentioned the societies for child psychology. Recently one has been founded in Germany, others before this time have been at work in England and America.

A whole series of investigations carried out in Kraepelin's laboratory in Heidelberg are of the greatest value for determining what the brain can do in the way of work and impressions.

An English specialist has maintained that the future, thanks to the modern school system, will be able to get along without originally creative men, because the receptive activities of modern man will absorb the cooperative powers of the brain to the disadvantage of the productive powers. And even if this were not a universally valid statement but only expressed a physiological certainty, people will some day perhaps cease filing down man's brain by that sandpapering process called a school curriculum.

A champion of the transformation of pedagogy into a psycho-physiological science is to be found in Sweden in the person of Prof. Hjalmar Oehrwal who has discussed in his essays native and foreign discoveries in the field of psychology. One of his conclusions is that the so-called technical exercises, gymnastics, manual training, sloyd, and the like, are not, as they are erroneously called, a relaxation from mental overstrain by change in work, but simply a new form of brain fatigue. All work, he finds, done under conditions of fatigue is uneconomic whether one regards the quantity produced or its value as an exercise. Rest should be nothing more than rest, - freedom to do only what one wants to, or to do nothing at all. As to fear, he proves, following Binet's investigation in this subject, how corporal discipline, threats, and ridicule lead to cowardice; how all of these methods are to be rejected because they are depressing and tend to a diminution of energy. He shows, moreover, how fear can be overcome progressively, by strengthening the nervous system and in that way strengthening the character. This result comes about partly when all unnecessary terrorising is avoided, partly when children are accustomed to bear calmly and quietly the inevitable unpleasantnesses of danger.

Prof. Axel Key's investigations on school children have won international recognition. In Sweden they have supplied the most significant material up to the present time for determining the influence of studies on physical development and the results of intellectual overstrain.

It is to be hoped that when through empirical investigation we begin to get acquainted with the real nature of children, the school and the home will be freed from absurd notions about the character and needs of the child, those absurd notions which now cause painful cases of physical and psychical maltreatment, still called by conscientious and thinking human beings in schools and in homes, education.